INDIGENOUS HISTORY FROM 1978–PRESENT
THE CONTEMPORARY ERA

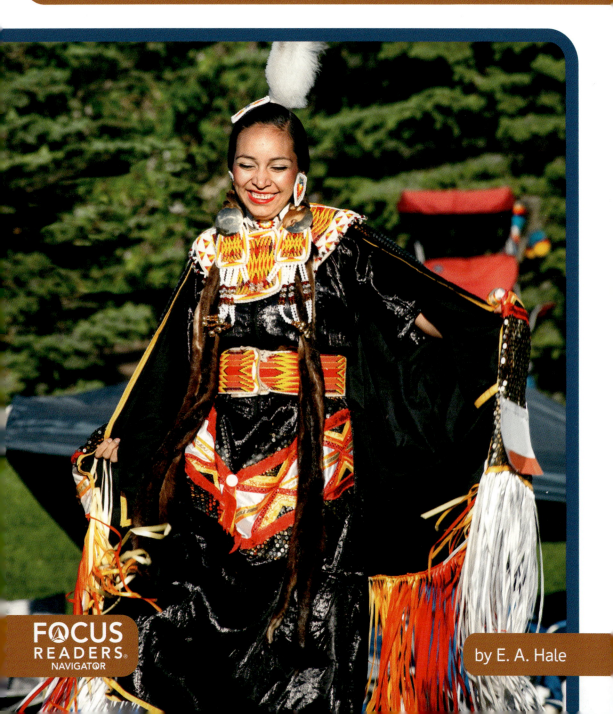

by E. A. Hale

FOCUS READERS®
NAVIGATOR

WWW.FOCUSREADERS.COM

Copyright © 2025 by Focus Readers®, Mendota Heights, MN 55120. All rights reserved. No part of this book may be reproduced or utilized in any form or by any means without written permission from the publisher.

Focus Readers is distributed by North Star Editions:
sales@northstareditions.com | 888-417-0195

Produced for Focus Readers by Red Line Editorial.

Content Consultant: Katrina Phillips, PhD, Red Cliff Band of Lake Superior Ojibwe, Associate Professor of History, Macalester College

Photographs ©: iStockphoto, cover, 1, 6; Wally McNamee/Corbis Historical/Getty Images, 4–5; Paul Connors/AP Images, 9; James Poulson/Daily Sitka Sentinel/AP Images, 10–11; Shutterstock Images, 13; Lindsey Wasson/AP Images, 15; Paul Morigi/The Smithsonian's National Museum of the American Indian/AP Images, 17; Don Ryan/AP Images, 18–19; Seth Wenig/AP Images, 21; Ann Heisenfelt/AP Images, 23; Kevin Dietsch/Getty Images News/Getty Images, 24–25; Red Line Editorial, 27; Terray Sylvester/VWPics/AP Images, 28

Library of Congress Cataloging-in-Publication Data
Library of Congress Cataloging-in-Publication Data is available on the Library of Congress website.

ISBN
979-8-88998-416-0 (hardcover)
979-8-88998-444-3 (paperback)
979-8-88998-496-2 (ebook pdf)
979-8-88998-472-6 (hosted ebook)

Printed in the United States of America
Mankato, MN
012025

ABOUT THE TERMINOLOGY

The terms **American Indians** and **Native Americans** are used interchangeably throughout this book. With more than 570 federally recognized tribes or nations in the United States, the usage will vary. Native nations and their people may use either term. The term **Indigenous peoples** describes groups of people who have lived in an area since prehistory. It may also be used as a shorter term to describe the federal designation **American Indians, Alaska Natives, and Native Hawaiians**.

ABOUT THE AUTHOR

E. A. Hale is a proud member of the Choctaw Nation of Oklahoma.

TABLE OF CONTENTS

CHAPTER 1

Indigenous Laws 5

CHAPTER 2

Giving Honor 11

VOICES FROM THE PAST

Wampum Belts 16

CHAPTER 3

Indigenous Efforts 19

CHAPTER 4

Progress 25

Focus Questions • 30
Glossary • 31
To Learn More • 32
Index • 32

CHAPTER 1

INDIGENOUS LAWS

For years, US laws and actions often tried to decrease the power of Native nations. However, protests led by Native people pushed against this. One march was the Longest Walk in 1978. Activists focused on Native rights and **sovereignty**. They were treated better than people who walked the Trail of Broken Treaties

The Longest Walk began in California in 1978. More than 2,000 people went to Washington, DC.

The Indian Child Welfare Act took care of tribal members and their cultures.

in 1972. Then, protesters wanted to fix years of unfair US policies toward Native nations. They took over a federal building. Police arrested them. But both the 1972 and 1978 protests led to many changes.

These changes often took the form of new laws. The laws helped protect Native people. Congress passed three important laws in 1978. The first was the Indian Child Welfare Act. The act kept Native children safe. It said they had rights. Their parents and tribes had rights, too. All states had to follow this law.

Congress also passed the American Indian Religious Freedom Act that year. This law protected Native religions. Native people were free to worship in their own ways. The act let them use **sacred** things for ceremonies. They could worship at special sites, too. No state could stop them from these tribal actions.

The Tribally Controlled Community College Assistance Act also passed in 1978. The act gave each tribe funds to run its own tribal college. It provided more opportunities for Native students. In 1988, Congress passed the Indian Gaming Regulatory Act. It let sovereign

SACRED OBJECTS

Before the United States formed, sovereign nations had sacred **rites** and rituals. Peyote cactus is a plant used for some Native religions. But it was outlawed for years. Then Congress changed the American Indian Religious Freedom Act in 1994. It made peyote legal. Eagle feathers or bones could now be used in sacred ways, too. Laws had protected bald eagles and golden eagles from harm. Today, non-Natives may not own parts from these eagles. Native people may have them but cannot sell them.

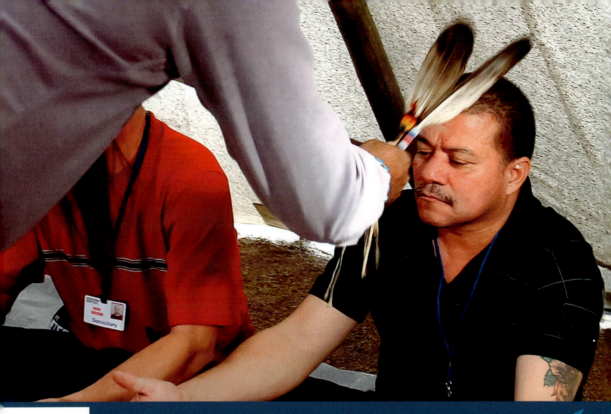

Eagle feathers are important for many Native ceremonies.

nations run gaming, or gambling, businesses on tribal lands. Gambling is when people bet money on a game. Both tribes and the states earn money from gaming. Gaming helps support school programs, childcare, food, housing, health care, and more.

CHAPTER 2

GIVING HONOR

Sacred Native items had often been stolen. Sometimes grave robbers dug up Native graves. They took bones or **artifacts** to study. Native people fought to bring back lost items and ancestors.

For example, the Smithsonian Institution had collected or taken thousands of Native remains. Tribes

In 2005, the Smithsonian Institution returned a sacred Killer Whale hat to Tlingit leader Mark Jacobs Jr.

asked for them back. This helped lead to a law in 1989. The Smithsonian had to return some sacred objects. The law also set up a new museum. It was called the National Museum of the American Indian. The museum is part of the Smithsonian. It shows histories, arts, and cultures of Native people in the United States.

In 1990, Congress passed more laws for Native people. One was the Native American Graves Protection and **Repatriation** Act (NAGPRA). The law gave tribes the right to get back their own sacred objects. Many tribes held ceremonies. They decided their own ways to rebury bones on tribal lands.

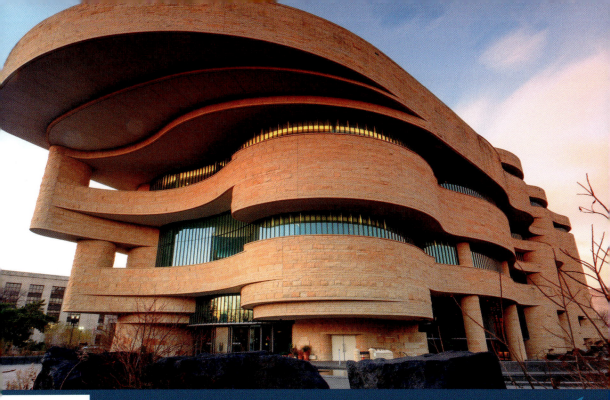

The National Museum of the American Indian opened in 2004 in Washington, DC.

Congress also passed the Native American Languages Act in 1990. The law gave all people the right to learn and speak a Native language. Congress added to the law in 1992. This change provided funds to Native nations so they could teach these languages. Learning to speak their own languages made people proud of their past.

Native people have long **advocated** for recognition. In 1990, Congress started National Native American Heritage Month. It honors all Native people in the United States. Each November, many tribes hold special events.

The first Indigenous Peoples' Day was celebrated in 1992. It became a holiday in many cities and states. It is often celebrated in place of Columbus Day. Christopher Columbus came to North America in 1492. But sovereign tribes of Native people have lived there for thousands of years.

One movement to protect Native people is often called Missing and Murdered Indigenous Women.

Since 1994, Congress has passed other laws to protect Indigenous people. The Violence Against Women Act gave tribes more power to fight crime. Two more laws passed in 2020. Savanna's Act created an online tool. It helped tribal police track down missing and murdered Indigenous people. The Not Invisible Act aimed to fight violence against Native people.

VOICES FROM THE PAST

WAMPUM BELTS

The passing of NAGPRA had a major impact. Tribes got back items taken a long time ago. In 2009, three non-Native brothers tried to sell two **wampum** belts. They wanted thousands of dollars.

The Haudenosaunee Confederacy of six Native nations took action. Its members claimed the belts were owned by their ancestors. They said the belts still carried Native culture. Bradley Powless is part of the Eel Clan of the Onondaga Nation. He described the importance of the belts in 2014. Wampum, he said, "records our history. . . . The belts are a great way to remind the speaker what actually happened a long, long time ago."[1]

It was hard to prove the Native nations' case. But the tribes did not give up. They dug through old records. They read old letters from the early buyers. Native scholars showed timelines. They showed which tribes the belts belonged to.

Wampum was never meant to be used as money or sold for money. The belts were not art for sale.

The three brothers had wanted cash from a sale. But then one brother died in 2017. The other two brothers changed their minds. They gave both wampum belts back to the tribes.

1. Bradley Powless, Eel Clan. "What Is Wampum?" *New York State Museum*. New York State Museum, n.d. Web. 12 June 2024.

CHAPTER 3

INDIGENOUS EFFORTS

Native nations continue to advocate for their rights and sovereignty. Tribes celebrate and highlight their cultures. They find ways to honor and help their people. Tribal members speak out for laws to make the United States better.

In 1998, a new group formed. It was called the American Indian Alaska Native

> **Learning the language of their ancestors is important to many Native people.**

Tourism Association. It was started by tribes for tribes. The group built up tourism. It helped people from across the globe visit Native lands. Tourism brings in money to Native nations.

The 2008 Code Talkers Recognition Act honored Native war heroes. Native soldiers used their languages during World War I (1914–1918) and World War II (1939–1945). They sent codes to help win battles. The enemy did not know what their words meant. The US government gave medals to each Native nation with a code talker.

Native nations also focus on their citizens' health. Not all tribal members

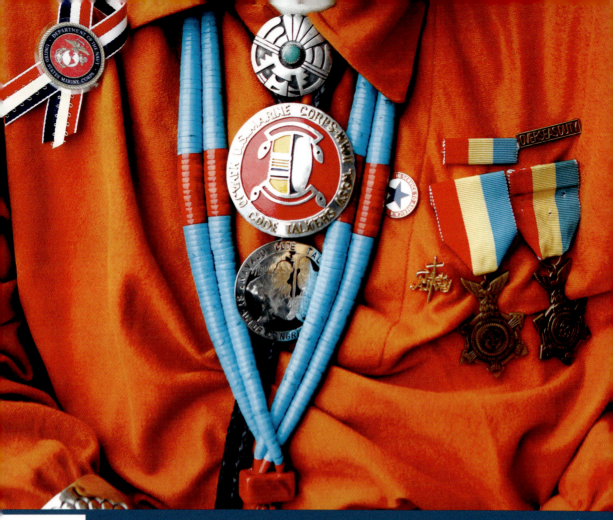

Each tribe and each code talker's family got its own medal. The Navajo Nation had the most code talkers.

have access to good food and health care. Many scientists study diseases that have impacted Native people. Diabetes has long been one of the big health problems.

In 2010, Congress passed an act to help. It funded aid for some needs of Native people.

States began to ban Native **mascots** for public schools in 2012. Some mascots

UNFAIR MASCOTS

Many schools chose mascots a long time ago. Back then, Native people felt the sting of **discrimination** in many areas. Native mascots often looked like cartoons. Later, school mascots drew anger, protests, and lawsuits. Some Native nations did not wait for laws to force changes. For example, in 2006, the Cherokee Nation took action. It worked with a nearby college. The school agreed to change its mascot. It went from the Redmen to the RiverHawks.

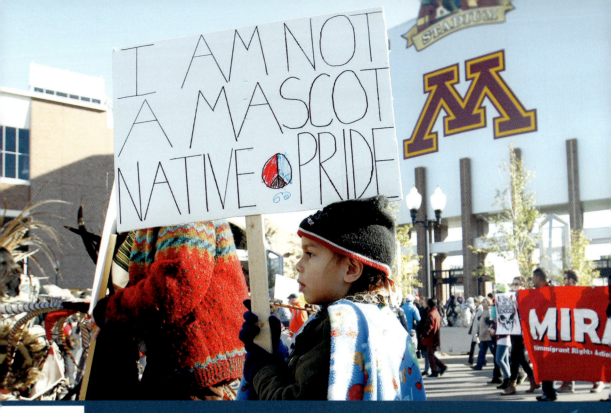

Protests from Indigenous people helped convince many schools and teams to change their mascots.

did not show respect. Some made fun of Native people and their cultures. A mascot face might be made to look silly. Or it might look less than human. Oregon was the first state to pass a law to ban some mascots. Later, professional sports teams changed mascots, too.

23

CHAPTER 4

PROGRESS

The US government made many treaties with Native nations. But the government has often failed to uphold them. As a result, Native nations have lost a great deal. But Native nations have always pushed for tribal sovereignty and rights.

In 2021, Deb Haaland became US secretary of the interior. She was the first Indigenous person to serve in the US Cabinet.

Sometimes Native nations have to take their cases to the court system. One case is known as *McGirt v. Oklahoma*. The US Supreme Court decided this case in 2020. The case focused on Muscogee (Creek) tribal land in Oklahoma. The court ruled the tribal land was still **reservation** land. The decision showed that old treaties are binding.

The US government also addresses other harms. In 2022, it released a report on federal Indian boarding schools. The report showed the harms from boarding schools from 1819 to 1969. School staff tried to wipe out Native cultures. They took children far from their homes.

Teachers forced children to speak English. Many children died at the schools. There are grave sites at more than 50 schools.

INDIAN BOARDING SCHOOLS

In 2022, the US government released a report about 408 Indian boarding schools between 1819 and 1969. This map shows how many of those schools were in each state.

 In 2016, the Standing Rock Sioux Tribe hosted many thousands of people to protest the Dakota Access Pipeline.

Tribes and governments still have conflicts. They are often over land or water rights. Tribes have sued over oil drilling on their land. They have sued over mining near sacred sites. They have sued and protested because of pipelines.

In recent years, Native nations have brought in billions of dollars to states.

Books, movies, and TV shows featured Native people and places. Congress passed the Native American Tourism and Improving Visitor Experience Act (NATIVE Act) in 2016. It boosted travel to lands owned by tribes. Native nations continue to work hard to build up their right to self-govern.

HAWAI'I

Tourism is the main industry in Hawai'i. The state has a volunteer program. Native Hawaiian educators let tourists work for free on the islands. In return, the educators teach tourists about the Native culture. Tourists may pull weeds or plant native plants. They help restore the Native land.

FOCUS QUESTIONS

Write your answers on a separate piece of paper.

1. Write a paragraph summarizing the laws mentioned in Chapter 2.

2. Why do you think Native nations want their historic items back from museums?

3. What did new laws force some schools to change?

    A. mascots
    B. colors
    C. cities

4. Why do some tribes work hard to attract tourists?

    A. Tribes do not want non-Native people to visit.
    B. Tourism can bring in money to tribes.
    C. Some tourists damage sacred Indigenous sites.

Answer key on page 32.

GLOSSARY

advocated
Supported a specific idea.

artifacts
Ancient objects made by humans.

discrimination
Unfair treatment based on people's looks or background.

mascots
Figures used to represent schools and sports teams.

repatriation
Returning people's remains to the original place where they belonged when living.

reservation
Land set aside by the US government for a Native nation.

rites
Words or actions performed as part of a religion.

sacred
Holy or pure.

sovereignty
The power to make rules and decisions without being controlled by another country.

wampum
Purple and white shells strung and woven into strands or narrow strips.

TO LEARN MORE

BOOKS

Bunten, Alexis. *What Your Ribbon Skirt Means to Me: Deb Haaland's Historic Inauguration*. New York: Hachette Book Group, 2023.

Newman, Patricia. *A River's Gifts: The Mighty Elwha River Reborn*. Minneapolis: Millbrook Press, 2023.

Rogers, Kim. *I Am Osage: How Clarence Tinker Became the First Native American Major General*. New York: HarperCollins Publishers, 2024.

NOTE TO EDUCATORS

Visit **www.focusreaders.com** to find lesson plans, activities, links, and other resources related to this title.

INDEX

boarding schools, 26–27

code talkers, 20

Haudenosaunee Confederacy, 16–17
Hawai'i, 29
health, 9, 20–21

Indian Child Welfare Act, 7
Indigenous Peoples' Day, 14

Longest Walk, 5

mascots, 22–23
McGirt v. Oklahoma, 26
missing and murdered Indigenous people, 15
Muscogee (Creek) Nation, 26

National Museum of the American Indian, 12

Native American Graves Protection and Repatriation Act (NAGPRA), 12, 16
Native languages, 13–14, 20
Native religions, 7–8

Powless, Bradley, 16

tourism, 19–20, 29
Trail of Broken Treaties, 5

Answer Key: 1. Answers will vary; 2. Answers will vary; 3. A; 4. B